Daring to Hope at the Cliff's Edge

ADVANCE COMMENTS FOR DARING TO HOPE AT THE CLIFF'S EDGE

Daring to Hope at the Cliff's Edge …is…timeless and timely, ancestral and modern, serious and whimsical. Be prepared for a journey of the moral imagination, an invitation into a council of all beings, and a unique experience that will leave you inspired, moved, and daring to hope.

—Della Duncan
Ecological Economist
Work that Reconnects Facilitator

Joggins Fossil Cliffs on the Bay of Fundy is the important geological focus for this engaging poetic meditation on our endangered earth. In Elizabeth Glenn-Copeland's lyrical treatment myth, Indigenous lore, geological science, song, storytelling, current events, and even pop culture intermingle in an impassioned search for understanding and for hope.

—Glen Sorestad
First Poet Laureate of Saskatchewan

As a cultural geographer specializing in the field of Education for Sustainable Development, I have witnessed the pivotal role the arts play in providing a holistic framework through which we can process our collective fears of the future. In this powerful narrative poem, Elizabeth takes us to the cliff's edge of these fears, and using pathos, humour and her unique wit, provides us with a personal model for resilient action.

—Dr. Michael Fox
Professor of Geography & Environment
Mount Allison University

Indigenous stories have carried memories across thousands of years, telling of people, places, and events through intricate woven words and spirits. Today, many scholars and communities work to decolonize hearts and minds through stories woven through Indigenous and settler voices, the practice of what a Mi'kmaq Elder calls Two Eyed Seeing. This engaging narrative is a welcome addition to emerging works acknowledging a need for understanding and healing in a colonized world. This poetic story is a must-read for anyone who struggles to activate hope for the future.

—Dr. Paulette Steeves
Associate Professor of History
Algoma University

Such scope! The scene painting and the imaginative flights that take to the skies in those scenes are (along with the stumbles) thoroughly engaging and moving. Wonderful sense of colour. The poems bring in aboriginal and ancient culture and myth, as they observe the various times of year and contemplate mother earth. It all makes for a powerful reading experience.

—Allan Briesmaster
Poet and Publisher

Daring to Hope at the Cliff's Edge

Pangea's Dream Remembered: A Poetic Odyssey

Elizabeth Glenn-Copeland

Chapel Street Editions

in association with

Joggins Fossil Institute

Copyright © 2019 by Elizabeth Glenn-Copeland
All rights reserved

Published by Chapel Street Editions in association with Joggins Fossil Institute

Chapel Street Editions
150 Chapel Street
Woodstock, New Brunswick E7M 1H4
www.chapelstreeteditions.com

Joggins Fossil Institute
100 Main Street
Joggins, Nova Scotia B0L 1A0
jogginsfossilcliffs.net/institute

Chapel Street Editions gratefully acknowledges Joggins Fossil Institute and the Municipality of Cumberland County (Nova Scotia) for their financial contribution to the cost of publishing this book.

ISBN 978-1-988299-23-5

Library and Archives Canada Cataloguing in Publication

Title: Daring to hope at the cliff's edge : Pangea's dream remembered, a poetic odyssey / Elizabeth Glenn-Copeland.
Other titles: Pangea's dream remembered, a poetic odyssey
Names: Glenn-Copeland, Elizabeth, 1957– author.
Description: A poem. | Includes bibliographical references.
Identifiers: Canadiana 20190099399 | ISBN 9781988299235 (softcover)
Classification: LCC PS8605.O6794 D34 2019 | DDC C811/.6—dc23

Cover photograph courtesy of Joggins Fossil Institute

Book design by Brendan Helmuth

Dedicated to Sophie, Eryn, Sorcha, Amy, Cas
and all the young people I have had the honour of collaborating with over the years
who have approached me with a question for which I have never been able to
provide a meaningful answer…

"We hear the Earth is dying
and we want to know,
why aren't the adults doing anything?"

TABLE OF CONTENTS

Foreword i
Preface iii
Pangea and the Joggins Fossil Cliffs v
Map of Joggins Region vi
Joggins Fossil Institute vii
    The Cliffs and the ArtScape Program vii
    Connecting Science and Art vii

DARING TO HOPE AT THE CLIFF'S EDGE 1

PROLOGUE
    Dragonfly's Tale 5

Part I: RIPTIDE SUPPLICATIONS
    Rock 9
    Autumnal Equinox 10
    Second Day of the Roman Festival of Mania 13
    Runic Half-Month of Wynn Commences 15
    Samhain 16
    Remembrance Day 19
    National Day of Remembrance & Action on Violence Against Women . 21
    Winter Solstice 23

Part II: THE LANGUAGE OF THE BIRDS
    Celtic Festival of Imbolc 28
    Spring Equinox 31
    Earth Day 34
    Festival Day of Beltane 35

Part III: WELCOMING THE UPSTART SPRING

Mother's Day 39
Lawns and Order 40
Letter to Rachel on Her Birthday 41
Silent Summer: An Ode to the Pollinators 42
Breaking News! 2018 Hurricane Season Commences Early 44
Summer Solstice Sabbat 45

Part IV: INTO THE MIST: A Midsummer Night's Odyssey 49

Part V: A REBIRTH OF WONDER

Harvest Festival of Lammas 65
The Mabon 67
Epilogue 69

AFTERWORD

Rapallo, Italy 73
Lamentation for Water 74
Kluscap's Sorrow 75
Seven Generation Thinking 76
Wind in the Sky 77

Guest Poets of the Joggins Project

Undercurrents 81
At the Torn Edge 82
Joggins, Thirty-One Years On 83

Acknowledgements 85
About the Author 87
Selected References 88

FOREWORD

The setting of this narrative poem is the majestic Joggins Fossil Cliffs—a paleontological wonder on the Bay of Fundy featuring three hundred million-year-old rocks that date back to the time paleontologists refer to as the Carboniferous Era. A few years ago, I came to know more about Joggins and its remarkable Fossil Centre through the latter's partnership with the Department of English at Mount Allison University, the goal of which was to align literary studies, ecology, and paleontology to explore relationships between facts and artefacts, between faithfully narrating the past and thoughtfully influencing the future. This kind of forward-thinking collaboration between art and ecological science is precisely what gave birth to the new poetic genre of ecopoetry in our culture at large, and it is a fresh example of ecopoetry that you now hold in your hands.

Ecopoetry is an essential ingredient in navigating our response to the world's current predicament because it contains the power to shift our minds out of the consensus-trance that marks our moment. Though the reasons may be legion, our culture is sleep-walking into the future, and where facts may fail, ecopoety can intervene, reminding us of what we know deep down to be true: that it is wrong to ransack nature for the fleeting sensations of luxury, and that true wealth consists only in such intangible goods as can be passed down to the seventh generation and beyond. This book offers just such a wake-up call, and like all good ecopoetry, it does so in uniquely powerful ways that we can trace in this case not only to its remarkable setting, but also to its author.

Elizabeth Glenn-Copeland is one of our wise women. She is a career artist committed to community-level change who has given her life to developing and generously sharing her creative gifts despite living in a culture that often devalues artists who do not follow the mainstream. I first met Elizabeth as a "non-traditional student" at Mount Allison University, a label that in her case meant a student whose rich life-experience makes her as much a colleague of the professor as a co-learner. As part of a group that included Canadian playwright Sharon Pollock, I mentored the development of her riveting spoken-word drama

"Bearing Witness," and then, a few months later, I worked with her on the "Earth Warriors Theatre Project." The latter was presented as a curriculum enrichment at our local middle school, and using the tenets of applied theatre, students explored the eco-despair they feel while summoning the collective courage required to face the crisis that is their future. Watching these youth not only perform brilliantly in front of a standing room only house but seeing their grit as they challenged the adults in the room to "Do Something!" brought to mind the guidance of American scientist Carl Sagan when he said, "Anything else you're interested in is not going to happen if you can't breathe the air and drink the water. Don't sit this one out." For these and other interventions in our community, Elizabeth won the 2018 Environmental Leadership Award, offering us tangible evidence of the power of art to transform our future.

At one point in our many discussions of art and life, Elizabeth suggested that ecopoetry consists of three principal ingredients: witness, wisdom, and warning. Witness invokes both a scientific capacity for accurate observation and the ethical imperative to "bear witness," to give voice to otherwise silent evidence in the court of human inquiry. Wisdom denotes the personal maturity of the speaker, including a willingness to set ego aside in favour of being a conduit for the accumulated insight of our ancestors. And warning, as this poem amply demonstrates, is an element best delivered not by any finger-wagging human (such as we encounter on social media), but rather by humanity's many fellow-travellers on earth's journey through time, including (in this case) the rocks of Joggins themselves.

There is, however, a fourth ingredient to ecopoetry that I would add to Elizabeth's trio, and that is wit. With roots in the Old English *"witan"* (to know), wit carries the connotations of both savvy insight and clever humour. Both are on offer in this poem, not least in the lovable character of the speaker herself, with her relatable fallibility and her humility in the face of mishap. Laughter, as they say, is the best medicine, especially when the times call for medicines whose principal ingredients are very bitter herbs indeed.

May this book be just such ecopoetical medicine. May it help us to heal and to dare to hope. May it reach that place within us where there abides a vision of what author and philosopher Charles Eisenstein calls "the more beautiful world our hearts know is possible."

Dr. Robert Lapp
Professor of English
Mount Allison University

PREFACE

I have long had a passion for communicating with the non-literate, animate world that began in childhood in the comforting embrace of an old Weeping Willow. Though we did not communicate with words, her wise counsel and abiding love saw me through difficult times I believe I may not have otherwise survived. So when I was offered a writing residency at Joggins, I jumped at the chance to spend time in the presence of the three-hundred-million-year-old rock formation known to the Mi'kmaq as *The Grand Nyjagon*. So began an incredible odyssey that took me down into the dungeon of my own eco-despair and forced me to examine what it really means to practice what Buddhist eco-philosopher Joanna Macy calls *Active Hope*.

Our beloved Earth is suffering a massive systems failure, commonly referred to in the abstract as *climate change*. It is through the blundering of our kind that we find ourselves in these desperate straits, and here specifically I refer to those of us who live in relative comfort free of the threat of war or drought or any of the myriad great sufferings that impact the majority of the people on this planet. Some have dubbed this epoch the *Anthropocene*, but perhaps a more apt name might be the *Pyrocene*, as our addiction to fossil fuels heat the world to the cliff's edge of doom for our kind, and sadly, many other species as well.

We are witnessing a rapid rise in a mental health condition now known as *eco-anxiety*. Dominant culture would have us believe that these fear-based anxieties are individual problems, and yet is not the evolutionary purpose of fear to notify us that there is danger present? Instead of suppressing these fears with shopping, can we come together to engage the best of our collective will to forge a new way?

I believe the portal to this new way lies partly in our DNA. On a cellular level, we all hold memories of living in harmony with the natural world. We can activate these memories in many way: through our imaginations; through time spent quietly in wild places; through the study of ancient, land-based wisdom; through wholehearted, community-driven, research-based exploration rooted in respect for the living world.

Evolutionary systems scientist, David Loye tells us in the *The Descent of Man* that Charles Darwin mentioned the word *Love* no less than ninety-five times (along with other feeling words like *Altruism and Sympathy*). For one hundred and sixty years mainstream science chose to ignore Darwin's moral theorizing in favour of a dangerously deadening paradigm that casts the Earth in the role of 'stage' on which we, the master species, can enact our dramas. But today we have an opportunity to change that paradigm, to choose to act from *Love*. And here I am not referring to a gushy *stay positive while avoiding looking straight into the eyes of the beast* sentimentalism. I am talking about realizing and advancing a potential of our evolutionary heritage, about a grateful and wholehearted embrace of our species embeddedness in the commonwealth of life and a fierce determination to defend and help nurture the beauty and integrity of the organic world.

This is a once in an epoch opportunity, my friends! *Will we wake up in time to salvage a future for the next seven generations? What part will you play in the unfolding story of this, humanity's next great adventure?*

I will leave you with the words of Second Century Sage, Hillel the Elder, "If not you, who? If not now, when?"

With you in solidarity,
Elizabeth Glenn-Copeland

PANGEA AND THE JOGGINS FOSSIL CLIFFS

Pangea is Greek for *One Earth*. Pangea is also the name of the supercontinent that existed during the late Paleozoic and early Mesozoic Eras. Driven together by Earth's tectonic forces, Pangea contained most of the continental landmasses we know today.

The area now known as Joggins Fossil Cliffs, situated along the 49th Parallel on the Bay of Fundy in Atlantic Canada, was a part of Pangea during the Carboniferous Period, approximately three-hundred million years ago. This land was equatorial rainforest surrounded by the Tethys and Panthalassa Seas. Originally called *Grand Nyjagon* by its first peoples, the Mi'kmaq, it was renamed *Chegoggins* meaning *Great Fish Weir* or *Great Encampment* and later changed by the Acadians to *Joggins*.

We acknowledge that the Joggins Fossil Institute stands on the unceded ancestral homelands of the Mi'kmaq People.

MAP OF JOGGINS REGION

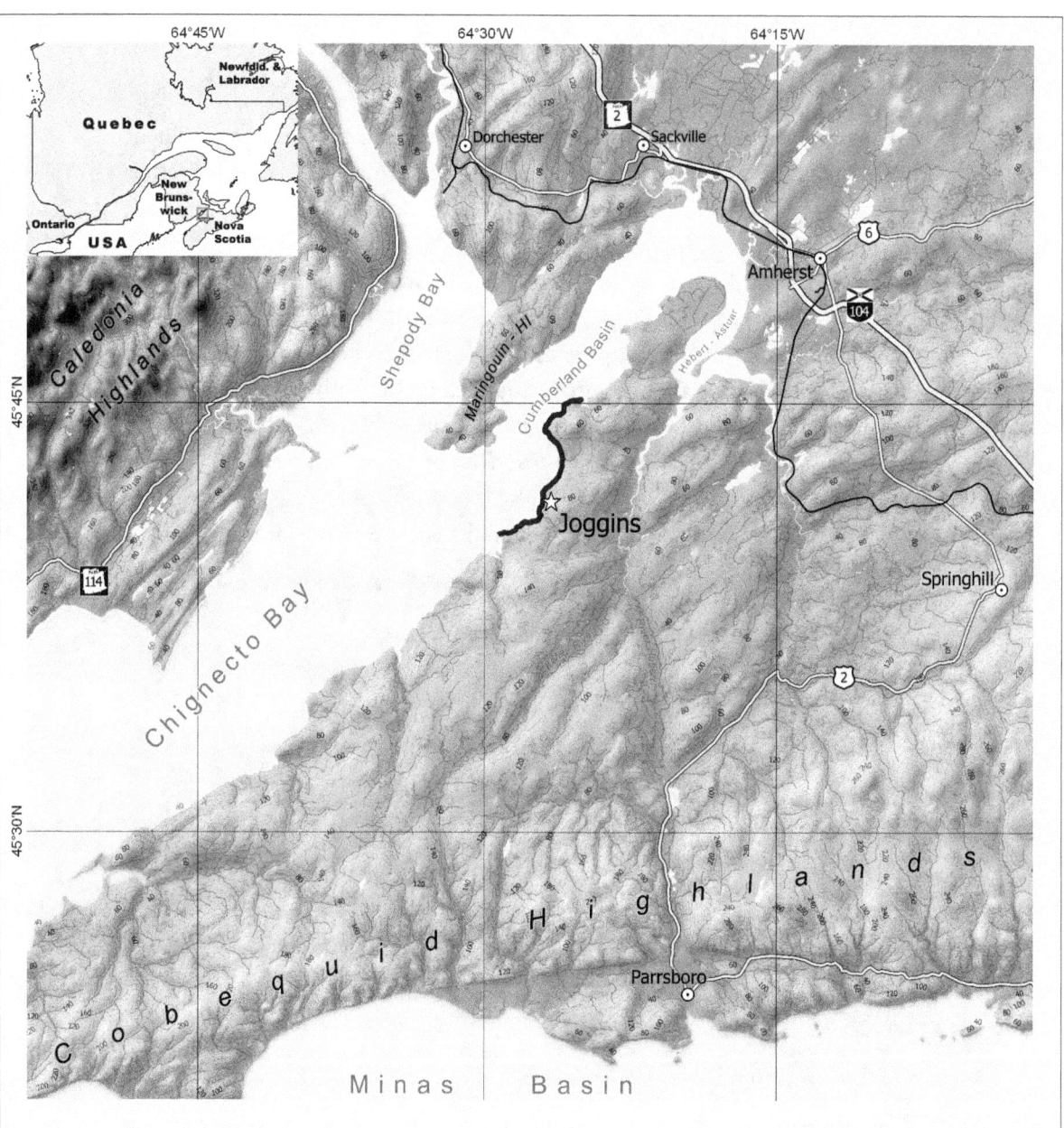

Physical geography of the Joggins area, western Cumberland County, Nova Scotia, and adjoining areas in New Brunswick with indication of the UNESCO World Heritage cliff section. Source: Wikimedia Commons. Map created by Gretarsson. https://commons.wikimedia.org/wiki/File:Joggins_regional_map_DE.png

JOGGINS FOSSIL INSTITUTE

The Cliffs and the ArtScape Program

The Joggins Fossil Institute is a not-for-profit charity and the governing body of Joggins Fossil Cliffs, a UNESCO World Heritage Site. Our mission is "to be exemplary in fulfilling our responsibilities, under the United Nations Convention for the Protection of World Cultural and National Heritage, to protect, conserve and present the outstanding value of the Joggins Fossil Cliffs through research, education and tourism."

In partial fulfillment of this mission, we created ArtScape; the Artist-In-Residence Program that invites international visual, literary, and performing artists to create art that engages with the natural environment and surroundings of the Joggins Fossil Cliffs. We chose Elizabeth Glenn-Copeland, a professional writer, theatre artist and artist facilitator as Artist-in-Residence for 2018 year. The selection jury was taken with her poetry, her commitment to community engagement and, in particular, her goal to explore what wisdom the 310 million-year-old Fossil Cliffs have to teach us in terms of our interconnectedness with all life.

We congratulate Elizabeth on the publication of *Daring to Hope at the Cliff's Edge: Pangea's Dream Remembered*. She has helped us realize one of our *dreams*—to bring Joggins Fossil Cliffs to the attention of new audiences.

Laurie Glenn-Norris, MA
Education and Outreach Manager
Joggins Fossil Cliffs Institute
November 13, 2018

Connecting Science and Art

As the Curator of Palaeontology at Joggins, I am responsible for the fossil collection housed here, exhibits, research, and creation of relevant educational material for students and visitors. I became interested in the interplay of science and art in my undergraduate days, but poetry was something that always eluded me. I am very much a "scientific writer" where allusion, alliteration and word play are rarely used.

Working with Elizabeth and listening to her poetry over the last year has given me a new perspective on the aesthetics and elegance that poetry can convey in ways no other form of writing achieves. *Daring to Hope at the Cliff's Edge* is an insightful, heartfelt and refreshing interpretation of the Joggins Fossil Cliffs' influence on science as well as our collective histories and imaginations.

Dr. Melissa Grey, PhD Geological Sciences
Curator of Palaeontology
Joggins Fossil Institute

DARING TO HOPE
AT THE CLIFF'S EDGE
PANGEA'S DREAM REMEMBERED

PROLOGUE

DRAGONFLY'S TALE

Once upon a time, when Earth was about to be born,

after she had slowly gestated in the fertile velvet of the Great Dreamers belly,

she careened out in a joyful arc

into the dark,

the silent dark,

the silent, starlit dark.

Around her were her brothers and sisters, Jupiter, Mars and Uranus,

Venus, Mercury and Saturn with her elegant, icy rings.

In the centre of them all was her Father, the Sun,

and Earth, overcome with gratitude for the beauty of her Life, began to cry.

She cried and cried and as she cried the Great Waters were created.

Magma too wanted in on the experiment, so he bubbled upwards

and in the cooling waters land was created.

Light sparked, and Earth knew that like her Mother, the Great Dreamer,

she too was gestating Life

in the dark,

the fertile dark,

the fertile velvet dark of her belly.

She birthed this Life into salty waters, and over eons it grew:

one cell to many to algae and plants, to flesh and blood and bone.

Propelled by the folding, warping, and fracturing of Earth's crust,

many continents became one and thus was born Pangea.

Here Earth dreamed a new dream and life began to flourish on land as it had in the seas.

This was the time when my ancestors, named by you as Megasecoptera, first appeared.

Wild winged and big as bobcats, in marshy stretches of equatorial rainforest we flourished.

We were Pangaea's dream.

Whose dream are you?

PART I

RIPTIDE SUPPLICATIONS

"We are living in a time of the convergence of multiple cataclysmic forces: runaway anthropogenic climate disruption, chronic wars, and the most grotesque economic equality ever witnessed on Earth…Racism, sexism, xenophobia and other structural forms of hate are amplifying around the globe as a fascist authoritarian has ascended to the U.S. presidency."

Dahr Jamail
Iraqi journalist

Frodo: "I wish none of this had ever happened."

Gandalf: "So do all who live to see such times but that is not for them to decide."

J.R.R. Tolkien
The Lord of the Rings

ROCK

you are called

an abiotic (non-living)

component of the ecosystem

(along with sunlight and clouds), but if that is so

why, when I am in your presence, am I am so moved?

I have read about you in books, observed you in various seasons,

talked about you in the abstract, but what if I could still my chattering mind

long enough to hear your voice? Your deep and abiding quietude lends such phenomenal

grace to this place that my breathing body longs to know you, to animatedly converse through

you with the Mystery of the Primordial Earth of which I am but an ever so small but critical part.

I am an earth-honouring woman of European descent. I am not native to this land.

Of my ancestral lineage with all Creation, I know little,

the knowledge I have gathered is pitifully small,

gleaned from books and old women

and pure dumb luck.

Like *Audre*, I know the Master's house cannot be razed with the master's tools.

Like *Richard*, I want to hear everything and nothing at the same time.

Like *Lawrence*, I am waiting for a rebirth of wonder.

Audre — African-American feminist poet and philosopher, Audre Lorde
Richard — Ojibwe author and journalist, Richard Wagamese
Lawrence — American beat poet, Lawrence Ferlinghetti

AUTUMNAL EQUINOX
September 22, 2017
Dark and Light in equal measure

Driving up the hill from River Hebert towards the cliffs at Joggins,

my thoughts are heavy from the constant undertow of anxiety that plagues my waking hours.

I awoke before first light to news of children in cages, centuries-old rages rising up.

Sirens scream, Syria burns, an old-growth forest is cut down to make toilet paper.

Markets thrive, species die,

the planet's oceans heat and rise.

Against this rising tide of mainstream malevolence, can anything I say or do matter?

Opening the car window, I inhale the perfume of grasses browning, leaves turning,

listen to the energetic medley of birdsong that is the dawn chorus.

An old black bear lumbers out of the bushes onto the two-lane road.

I slow to allow him time to cross. He pays me no mind,

disappears into a stand of poplar, spruce and gnarled jack pine.

Cresting the hill, I see that the village of Joggins still sleeps.

The parking lot at the Fossil Institute is empty.

Fat crimson rose-hips adorn the thicket of wild-rose bushes along the cliff's edge.

I walk the stone labyrinth under a sky streaked with ribbons of tangerine, purple, and grey.

Descending to the beach, the coastal wind, like me, is moody, raw.

A Sobeys' bag caught on a sharp-edged piece of driftwood makes a crackling, crinkling sound.

I rip it down, stuff it into my pocket,

try to banish the image of a whale washed up on the beach in Thailand: his guts full of plastic.

Dawn at the *Grand Nyjagon* and the beach is strangely still.

Fog hangs grey and heavy at the base of the cliffs as

millions of microscopic water droplets ascend slowly heavenward.

I watch a peregrine falcon circle overhead,

listen to the animated conversation of blue-black ravens huddled high on the fossil cliff,

see myself small in its shadow.

The tide is out; no water as far as the eye can see,

only small creeks like tiny capillaries fanning out into the fertile mud flats.

A flock of Laughing Gulls float gracefully on soft-grey, black-tipped wings.

A few dozen late-to-migrate piping plovers fly in perfect formation,

their under-wings flashing bronze as they plunge earthward to feast.

Soon they will begin their five thousand kilometre non-stop flight to South America.

I walk south towards Ragged Reef,

    past layers of three hundred million-year-old sedimentary rock

        set at a twenty degree angle by almost incomprehensible tectonic forces,

        trace the steps of Lyell, Dawson, and, by extension, Darwin;

founding fathers of the Earth Sciences that rocked the world with their upstart theories.

Light from the rising sun reflects gold on the cliff face that stands

        Silent

        Sombre

        Sublime

    I raise my arms high and wide.

Oh Ancient Cliffs,

Keeper of Primordial Wisdom…

You are Creation's Carboniferous Chronicle.

In the tradition of my ancestors, the Healers of Europe

who suffered the flames in a time ironically known as the Age of Enlightenment,

whose persecutions trained six generations of children to see those unlike themselves

as subhuman, those children once grown became

Conquerors

Colonizers

and look how well the training stuck…

SILENCE

In the tradition of all who honour Life as Sacred, I call out to

Sea and Sky,

Rock and Raven,

Fauna and Falcon,

Please…

SILENCE

Head bowed, I leave the beach, hot-faced and sorry.
Green bile burns holes in intestines slick and gruesome:
E-coli of the soul.

Must I forever ride inside this waking nightmare?

A bitter wind rises as I walk north to Downing Cove.
A Conspiracy of Ravens take wing.

SECOND DAY OF THE ROMAN FESTIVAL OF MANIA
October 5, 2017
The portal between this world and the Underworld is open

I return to the cliffs.

It is midmorning, and as the wind begins to rise,

the mighty Fundy shifts and sighs

as one hundred fifty billion tonnes of water, heavy with salt, ebbs and flows in common time.

Will I ever learn the subtle shifts in air and water that signal the turning of the tides?

In my pocket, my iphone buzzes.

I've got notifications!

I block out all stimuli: the hop-skip-hop of the wild sponge rolling down the beach,

                                  the laughter of the gulls as they wheel and dip in the grey-blue sky,

                                  the full-bodied bouquet of seaweed and salt and fertile decay.

I stare at the screen, hoping to receive tidings of great joy,

but instead see that   someone I don't know has responded to a comment

                        that someone else I don't know has commented on in a message

                        that someone I wish I didn't know has tagged me on

                        or is it in? Whatever.

Scrolling down, pictures of Royhingyan Muslims fleeing terror

                              POTUS throwing paper towels to hurricane victims

                              Kim showing off her new manicure to Kanye

                                                      I sweat shame.

High on the cliff's edge, drying goldenrod and saffron-coloured grass waltz in the breeze.

Anxious to accelerate accomplishment,
I join in the dance: not a waltz or a sway or a two-step, but a furious fandango,
executed in the style of highly successful white people who value speed over all.
My heart a dervish, my monkey mind whirling in a hundred different directions,
I clap, step, and skip my way over slippery stones,

> looking but not *seeing*,
>
> hearing but not *listening*,
>
> dancing faster and faster until my breath comes in scorching gasps.

Falcon cries high overhead, her marigold eyes flashing fire

Ghiii-ghiii-ghiiiiiiiiiii

Wisdom from Rilke slows me…

"Only when we tarry do we touch the holy."

I kick off my shoes, watch as they continue their frenzied jive south to Apple River.

Turning to face the cliffs, I kneel on stony sand,
needing physical pain to bring me down into my body.

A chattering fugue of fossil seekers moves onto the beach.
Dressed in warm gear and rain boots,
they are eager to decipher text written in rock from Lyell's Big Volume.
A little girl sees me kneeling, and probably thinking me an old woman beached,
runs to my aid. As she helps me to stand, she sings:

> *The more we stick together, together, together*
> *The more we stick together the happier we'll be.*

Out of the mouths of babes…

Can it be that simple?

RUNIC HALF-MONTH OF WYNN COMMENCES
October 13, 2017
The mystery of harmony within a disharmonious world is now manifest

The esoteric meaning of the runic letter *Wynn*

Perfection

Harmony

Hope

sometimes I'm *afraid* to hope

as if by hoping I commit to a process so terrifying that I might die in its discovery…

oh I can wax philosophical over coffee with friends, quote Rumi and Rilke, Oliver and Moore

but when I open the door in my belly to daylight so blinding that

my sight might be given back to me…

I wend my way along the Grand Exposure, walk inland through yellowing blades of grass.
Settling myself in a perfect circle of brown-gold needles at the foot of an old white pine,
I rest my head against the deep vertical grooves of her bark, look up through her branches,
catch sight of the ghost of the moon waning quietly in the pale blue sky.
Three black-capped chickadees flit from branch to branch.
I breathe in the comfort of their familiar whistle, their percussive *chick-a-dee-dee-deeeee*.
For their listening pleasure, I recite aloud my favourite Emily Dickinson poem…

"Hope is the thing with feathers—

That perches in the soul—

And sings the tune without the words—

And never stops—at all—"

I laugh out loud at the sight of three black-capped heads nodding as if in approval.

SAMHAIN
October 31, 2017
The veil between this world and the Otherworld is lifted

For over two thousand years, my Celtic ancestors celebrated the Festival of Samhain.

Believing that the dead returned to earth on this night,

they laid out banquet tables of food to fête the returning ancestors,

lit fires in ceremonies meant to ward off unwelcome spirits.

Perhaps my ancestral spirits will come to me tonight, offer counsel, teach me how to be.

I make my way down to the beach, dig a small ditch in the wet sand,

lay a fire with wood I gathered from my yard,

set a match to kindling I realize too late is too green to catch flame.

Clearly my ancestral memories do not include the basics of lighting a fire.

Dragons of indigo clouds drift inland.

The waxing gibbous moon looms malevolent in the darkening sky.

Time to go home.

I am gathering up my things when a murder of crows swoops overhead.

The wind begins to moan, and I hear—what?

> *A thundering of hooves?*
> *A gnashing of teeth like an angry Baba Yaga*
> *riding the night sky on her mortar and pestle?*

My rational mind tells me there was no strange sound, that it is only my imagination,

but none-the-less a *frisson* of fear snakes up my spine.

Wishing I'd brought a flashlight, I stumble towards the stairs, the moaning wind at my back.

The moaning modulates up an octave to a shrill shriek,

like the voice of actress Carol Kane but without the whimsy.

I want to run but find myself frozen in fear, and then...

| | *Knock, knock!* |

Am I losing my mind?
Or is this a Halloween remake of "A Christmas Carol"?

Knock, knock!

With hands on the side of my head
in the style of Munch's painting,
I open my mouth to scream.
No sound comes out.

Knock, knock!

Then up from the ground,
a basso voice…

Don't be frightened,
you flustered fool!

What or who is talking to me?

Knock, knock!

The voice again…

"It is the three strange angels.
Admit them! Admit them!"

The three strange angels?
Hell's bells! Could it be?

Just do as I say!
ADMIT THEM!

I admit I am terrified.
I admit I don't like being shouted at, even if it is by the inimitable D.H.* himself.
I admit I must do something or lose my mind.

Closing my eyes, I focus on the otherworldly sound,
visualize a door opening at the buckle of Orion's belt.

The knocking stops.
The wind blows still.

Opening my eyes, I see…
> The First Strange Angel as he steps out from behind the star named *ALNITAK*.
> Flexing his foot, he daintily points his toe, then shapeshifts into the trickster, Raven.
>> He flies towards me, almost invisible in the night sky,
>> to drop a purple-black feather at my feet.

> Second Strange Angel peeks shyly from behind the luminous *ALNILAM*.
> Executing a perfect tour jeté, she then morphs into a family of Laughing Gulls.
>> Diving earthwards, they each release feathers of pure white.
>> I catch them in my upturned palm.

> Third Strange Angel, having chosen one of the brightest stars in the sky, *MINTAKA*.
> Mimicing the lissome physicality of Nureyev, and soaring through the nebula,
>> he becomes Falcon, Solar Emblem of the Sun God, Ra.
>> After releasing two golden feathers, he disappears as if by magic.

The humpback moon, now seated in a lotus position,
casts just enough light for me to see my way to the steps.
But I do not move, do not want to break the spell.
Holding the three white feathers in my hand, I remain perfectly still.
Only when my body is shivering do I grudgingly recognize it is time to go.

Using a piece of dried kelp,
I tie together the sage gifts of my feathered friends, tuck them into my ponytail.

Thanking D. H., my winged friends, and those of my ancestral lineage who surely were here,
I ascend the stairs proudly, crowned with tangible evidence of Emily's Hope.

---

* D.H. Lawrence's poem, "Song of a Man Who Has Come Through" has been like a mentor to me lo these many years. I have excerpted a few lines from this work along with the imagery of the Three Strange Angels.

REMEMBRANCE DAY
November 11, 2017
Lest we forget

Under a bruised sky,

the mournful sound of *The Flowers of the Forest*,* more commonly known as Pipers Lament

sweeps up from the Joggins Cenotaph.

I envision a sea of humans bedecked with red poppies,

their faces fixed in expressions of mourning.

Under a bruised sky,

in the chill air, the Lament crescendos then fades as it has for decades across our land.

I flashback to 1967, to the Cenotaph in my home town,

    see my grandfather standing tall and proud in his uniform,

    his eyes red with unshed tears,

    see his hand shake as he pats his pocket,

    checking for the cigarette that would later calm his nerves.

Did his mind recoil as the music forced remembrance of the horrors of Ypres, the Somme, Passchendaele,

    the trenches, the searing nerve gas which ate away half his stomach, and then, when the

        "war to end all wars" was over, after he'd gone home to create a life,

            leaving his family to serve yet again when the threat of

                fascism reared its hateful head?

I remember how as a small child, I would follow him everywhere,

my little legs pumping to keep pace with his long-legged gait.

I remember his gruff kindness, the Scots brogue which got thicker after a few whiskies,

the way the tears would spill down his cheeks at the playing of "Bonnie Scotland."

But mostly I remember his hands with their long tapering tobacco-stained fingers,
hands that did not shy away from hard work, hands that

> tilled the soil that planted the seeds that reaped the harvest from the back-yard garden,
> that twirled the beaters that struck the drum that set the rhythm for marching feet,
> that gripped the mortar that fired the rifle that carried the bodies of fallen brothers,
> his hands, his beloved hands that   never
>   stopped
>   shaking.

Today my grandfather's spirit walks with me on the beach.
Together we feel the rhythm of the eternal tides,
note the inconstant constancy of the sea,
savour the *whoosh* of worrying winds,
reminding him of his cradle home
on the Firth of Forth where it
meets the North Sea.

In the charged silence following the Pipers Lament,
I kneel on cold sand, bow my head,
think of poppies and wreathes laid as Anne Frank's diary lies mouldering in a glass cage.

> *Oh Grandfather!*
> *We have broken faith with you,*
> *we willing consumers of franchised fascism*
> *who have swallowed promises written on ice.*

---

*"The Flowers of the Forest" is an old Scottish folk song that commemorates the Battle of Flodden in 1513 where seventeen thousand Scots sacrificed their lives attempting to free themselves from British rule.

NATIONAL DAY OF REMEMBRANCE & ACTION ON VIOLENCE AGAINST WOMEN

December. 6, 2017

Wear the White Ribbon

Rock knows that only when the tears flow can there be healing.

Say their names:

Geneviève Bergeron, Helene Colgan, Nathalie Croteau, Barbara Daigneault, Annie Turcotte, Anne-Marie Edward, Maud Haviernick, Barbara Klucznik-Widajewicz, Annie St-Arneault, Maryse Laganière, Maryse Leclair, Anne-Marie Lemay, Sonia Pelletier, Michèle Richard.

Ice underfoot makes the descent to the platform difficult,

the difficult descent into

this day.

Contemplate water.

This body of water with its high tides,

this Fundy with her fifty-seven foot high tides,

tides that surge like the blood in my veins,

these incoming tides, this tidal bore that rises like a wall of terrible wonder towards rock,

this body of rock, wearing her down wearing me down,

wearing and tearing at

my body.

Body.

From the old English *bodig*

meaning main or principal part of a thing.

Contemplate the body.

MY
BODY
is your body
are the bodies of children of the grandmothers the grandfathers
the forests the trees the rocks and seas the sky the ones with roots with wings with branches
with gills with tails with nowhere to go with those who know that what has been
deadened and dismissed as dirty is my body is the Earth's body
and the Earth's body is the body of the Mother
I am a mother your mother your daughter your father son and holy spirit
I the women raped the girl with genitals mutilated with pleasure eradicated left with only pain
pain in the body in the bodies the bodies of water of community of knowledge creating
bodies of hate bodies of suffering of you against me of apology instead of affirmation
the body politic crowning the heads of the puppet kings who respect nobody no body no no
NO is a powerful word but use it in defense of women and you are a bitch in defence of the land
you are an eco-terrorist in defence of a child a tree a family of wild things and you are
unhinged too emotional not reasonable not somebody no no
NO one body belongs to anybody and whose body gets to decide who is somebody oh
my body is your body are the bodies whose spirits will not be crushed by the nobodies
claiming to be somebody our bodies embody not the body politic but the body heretic the body apostate
because the body who embodies dissent is radical
radical meaning root roots of love roots of compassion roots of trees that hold the land together
roots of justice for all coloured bodies indigenous bodies female queer disabled bodies
bodies of wisdom long buried in the patriarchal mire of bodies banished burned bloodied
blood is the river of life and blood knows yes blood knows the tide is turning
YES blood knows bone knows yes rock knows yes breath knows
brash brave breath breathing beatific brilliance and
bloody hell can you be that body? can you please brave the fear to be that body
who embodies the brazen truth that
the body
mine, yours and that of the flowering elm are
SACRED

WINTER SOLSTICE
December 21, 2017
Honour the Goddess in her dark aspect

In the arched dome of a blue-black sky,
stars sing in the language of light,
a recitative of wonder.

In the molten womb of the planet's core,
magma drones in the language of fire,
druidic tomes of primal thunder.

This is the longest night.
The silent night.
Snowflakes dance downward,
making the dark night bright.

I inhale deeply, refreshing lungs too long full of stale, over-talked air.

Placing down my six feathered crown, I fall backwards into powdery white.
Lying still and strangely warm, the pulsing cadence of water, hued chocolate brown,
seems to speak to me of nightmares and hope
and the wholehearted knowing of eons-old ecstasy.

But the cliffs, crowned with coronets of ice,
stand silent still.

Oh Great Cliffs,
In what language will you speak?
How will I know your voice?

PART II

THE LANGUAGE OF THE BIRDS

"Birds played an important role in Indo-European religion, from the Renaissance, it was the inspiration for some magical priori languages, in particular musical languages…The symbolic meaning of the Raven in Native American Indian lore describes the raven as a creature of metamorphosis, and symbolizes change/transformation…In Sufism, the language of birds is a mystical language of angels."

Sonya Van Gelder
Connecting The Dots Of Our Ancient Past

The language of the birds
was considered a secret and perfect language in many alchemical traditions.
Though history has hidden the names of many of those who paid the price required to learn this magical tongue, some of their stories were hidden away in the folds of fairy tales,
as in this rendition of a classic tale from Old Russia.

Once upon a time there was a young man named Ivan who had a perfectly unselfish heart. He lived with his older brother, Dmitri and his Father, a proud and wealthy merchant. One fine spring day, Ivan's Father tells his sons to go out into the world to make their fortunes. The brothers set out and as night falls, they find themselves walking through a dark forest. Suddenly Ivan hears a cry of distress. He runs towards the sound and finds, at the base of a giant oak, a baby bird fallen from its nest. He gently picks up the still-blind creature, tucking it into his pocket, then scales to the top of the tree where he returns the baby to his Mother's nest. Overcome with gratitude, she offers to teach Ivan the language of the birds. Spring turns to summer and Ivan stays in the forest, intent on his learning. Only when the leaves turn from green to orange does he set out for home. Along the way he meets his brother who boasts of money and women and the name he made for himself at the gambling tables. Dmitri's face contorts into a sneer at the news of Ivan's puny exploits.

When the brothers arrive home, they proudly recount their stories. The Father orders a fine feast to be prepared for his eldest son, then banishes Ivan to the barn. As the moon rises high in the still night, an icy rain begins to fall. Shivering with cold and fear, Ivan hears the barn swallow tell him that all will be well, that one day he will save his brother from execution, rescue his Father from poverty, marry a clever princess, and become a wise and benevolent King.

Ivan's story has many twists and turns, replete with high adventure involving pirates and talking crows and I encourage you to read it in its entirety, but the upshot is this; when faced with trials, Ivan calls on his bird friends and thus saves himself and many others from great suffering.

The language of the birds
was considered a secret and perfect language in many alchemical traditions.
It was also known as the Green Language.

CELTIC FESTIVAL OF IMBOLC
February 1, 2018
Honour the seed which this day begins to burrow upwards through frozen earth towards the light

Today my country, once known for its enlightened socialism,
has given the nod to B.P. (of Deepwater Horizon fame)
to allow drilling near the protected lands of Sable Island.
This is sad news,
bad news for the Wild Horses that run wild on that protected strip of sand,
bad news for the Ipswich Sparrow for it is here, and only here, that they breed.
Oh, the Lords of Conquest are riding high, their silk suits stained with gravy!
Having struck their Faustian bargain,
they act as if they own the world,
which they do.

Raven's shrill scream jars me out of my dark ruminatings and back to the present.

The February wind is strong, her numbing gusts burn circles on my cheeks.
The tide is boring her way out, a rushing clamour moving west.
Over my blue-striped hat, I place my feathery crown,
pray that today it will act like an antennae,
that the cliffs will speak,
that I will understand.

Making a careful descent down the stairs on cleated boots, my breath is white vapour.

Rings of frost frozen on patches of seaweed dapple the beach with patterns of slate and silver.

Shivering in layers of down, I place my gloved hand on a rocky outcropping,
wish for a whisper of encouragement, and hear…

"No coward soul is mine,

No trembler in the world's storm-troubled sphere:

I see Heaven's glories shine,

And faith shines equal, arming me from fear."

                                                  Goddess bless Emily Brontë!

Emboldened, I begin again, humble myself at the base of the cliff,

make offerings to Sea and Sky…

Sage for wisdom

Lavender for beauty

Rue to acknowledge that Poison can be turned into Medicine.

Grandmothers of Stone and Sea,

I realize you have no reason to trust that I am not just another

attention-seeking, short-sighted two-legged,

and yes, I have been these things, but…

Unsure what next to say,

I take off my glove, run my fingers over my feathered antennae.

Should you require references,

can I direct you to the Weeping Willow who mothered me as a child?

I spent many hours in her embrace and she knows my heart best of anyone.

Light sprites waltz on foam crested waves.

Falcon sails resplendent on crested wing.

Oh Grandmothers,

sing to me in salt spray your songs of sorrow and joy, let me….

Raven cuts me off:

Oh holy night!!

If you want to hear anything of value you must STOP TALKING!

I stand stock still in shame at being chided so, but then…
Hey! How is it I understand what you are saying?!

Air whistles as Raven dives, turning skyward inches shy of my head.
Isn't that what you asked for, you dim-witted two-legged?
To understand the language of the birds?

I squat down,
dig my hands into cold sand,
settle down to wait.

Raven groans.
Waiting is not the same as listening.
You have merely placed your mind on hold.
Be still.
Like Heron waiting for her prey.

A wraith of fog pulls up her glamour.
Raven's wings flash amethyst in the now moon-lit sky.

I am listening.

SPRING EQUINOX
March 21, 2018
Light and Dark in equal measure

Fundy is donned in an almost Caribbean blue as preparation for Ēostre's day dawns bright and sunny.

Think egg.

Estrogen.

The fertility of bunnies.

I hip hop down the beach,

slightly manic due to the consumption of too many chocolate eggs.

After seven weeks of mindful listening, I am Peter Cottontail's wife in full and ecstatic estrus!

Sandstone, Siltstone and Shale!

On behalf of my kind, I need…

The shrieking of Raven high overhead overwhelms my voice.

Need, need, need!!

You humans, always coming to us with your never-ending needs!

The family of Laughing Gulls swoop low, make an offering of good luck: a dollop of gull poop.

It lands on my glasses, runs down my cheek.

Stifling the urge to gag, I wipe it away with the back of my glove.

Oh Great Cliffs,

I need…

The largest of the gulls interrupts:

Lord tunderin'! Don'tcha know anything about approachin' yer Elders, girl?!

She's three hunderd million years old, fer Gawd's sake!

Now take that dern feathery hat off and interduce yerself!

I do as I'm told.

My name is…is…

In a sweet voice, the smallest gull says:
'Scuse me, missus, but have ya brought us anyting ta nibble on?

I stammer:
I'm sorry, I don't have any food, but…
Hey, stop that!!

More poop: this time, from the whole family!
Trying to avoid the barrage, I blunder backwards, lose my balance,
land hard on knotwrack-covered stone.

The air rings with mocking laughter.
Oh la-dee-da, she's some funny, eh?!
What an arse!
Finally, some comedy!

Still flat on my back, I roll onto my side,
check to see if there are other humans on the beach to witness my shame.
When I see the coast is clear, I grab a handful of drying dulse, wipe my face clean.
With my nose still full of fishy smelling bird dung,
I find myself drawn to examine the knotwrack's tiny grape-like bladders,
marvel at the tracks of marine snails,
the grey-white barnacles,
the shiny sea stars.

I roll onto my back, see the outline of the crescent moon pale in the sky.

Sitting up, I return my feathered antennae to my head.

Falcon glides down from the rock ledge, landing on his sturdy yellow feet.
He arches his neck up, as if to show off his notched beak, his elegant eye rings.
We regard each other.
He cocks his head right, then left.
Eeee-chup!

I shake my head, not understanding.

Eeee-chup!
You are doing well. Don't give up!

A tide of euphoria floods me.
Falcon, the wanderer, the fastest bird on earth has spoken to *me*.

Thunder rumbles in the distance, rumbles then *craacks!*

Far out over the bay, a fork of lightening arcs from a purple-stained sky.
Then cumulonimbus lets go, first a drizzle, then a pewter-stained cascading curtain.

Like Tim Robbins in "The Shawshank Redemption",
I arch my back, open my arms wide, sing out my gratitude on a single sustained note.
The rain soaks through my clothes and into my pores.
I feel the cells in my body merge with some unnamed yet never-the-less intoxicating
Wonder.

I look to the cliffs and smile.

No longer estranged from my sensing body,
I have no answers, only
Reverence.

EARTH DAY
April 22, 2018
Honour Gaia, the Mother who has yet to reveal her Mysteries

Gossamer Mist rises violet, sings greetings to
    Moon as she sheds silver garments to disappear in
        Sky, now beaming blue, as he eagerly awaits his invited guests.

At mid-morning they appear, a crowd of laughing children.

The Laughing Gull family gives greeting then swings into action,
become a company of seasoned players, *squaawking* and *screeeching*,
wheeling and dipping in currents of spring-fresh air.
Before the children can tire of their antics, the Gulls intuitively move to the second act,
landing on the beach to play a game of *screeeaam* and chase!
As children and Gulls run north, then south, then north again, the parents,
not wanting to get mud on their shoes, stay huddled *en masse* at the base of the stairs,
shouting the perils of ruining good clothes.
As Sun finds his zenith in the sky, the gulls retreat to the cliffs for an afternoon siesta.
Cumulus clouds of puffed cotton gather, changing shapes as if on cue:
first a dragon, then a unicorn, then a lion proud and wild.
Parents and children gather to watch, crouched on the drying sand, their eyes wide as saucers.

Later, when the children have gone home, and the sun hangs heavy and red on the horizon,
I stand, extend my arms, remain perfectly still, wanting to feel
    the speed of Earth's rotation at a thousand miles per hour
        as she orbits around the sun at sixty seven thousand miles per hour
            in a Solar System that whirls through our Galaxy at
                four hundred and ninety thousand miles per hour.

                    Thank you, Mother Earth!!

FESTIVAL DAY OF BELTANE
May 1, 2018
Earth energies at their strongest

flooding down the cliff face, fresh water
streaming brightness

underfoot, rain-soaked algae glows green on the cliff face
sunburst lichen glistens titian yellow

I wash my face in morning dew
this day promises beauty

kicking off my shoes, I wiggle my toes in sun-warmed tide pool
dream a dream of maidens dancing round and round the Rowan tree
young men tease and tussle while
under a canopy of spring-green leaves new mothers nurse their babes
ssshing and *cooing*
cooing and rocking
sitting in the full sun, the old ones rub their tired bones contemplate what matters

as the dream fades, I peer with longing at the layers of rock

my heart leaps as I see, winging in from parts unknown and shimmering promise
my allies, the birds

the time is drawing nigh when your longing will be met
go home
gather your energy
you must be ready

PART III

WELCOMING THE UPSTART SPRING

"Nothing is so beautiful as spring—…"

Gerrard Manley Hopkins

MOTHER'S DAY
May 13, 2018

Grasses greening in my garden, wick rising, fantasizing

the blossoming beauty of   Crocus,

                                     Aconite,

                                     Hyacinth too!*

And on the greening forest floor   darling bells of blue.

Peepers singing in the marshlands, mesmerizing, energizing

the soaring songs of   Scarlet Tanager,

                                     Indigo Bunting,

                                     Rose-breasted Grosbeak too!**

And drying wings on wetland grass   a dragonfly birthed new.

Intent on enjoying this springtime glory,

I am settling myself in my favourite lakeside park when

(O Horror!) my senses are assaulted by the stink and buzz of   Blowers and Mowers

                                                                                                 Buzzers and Whippers

                                                                                                 Whackers too!

My tea grows cold as I watch a young man drive up and down in straight lines for hours on end.
He looks so happy, and I can't help but wonder…

Does riding a John Deere stir unconscious DNA memories of farming?
Or perhaps something more medieval involving horses and the glory of the charge?

                                                                   Oh the joys of lawns and order!

---

* Flowers that rise up through cold, hard earth bringing a teaching of perseverance.
** Songbirds who may not survive the sudden shifts in spring weather.

LAWNS AND ORDER*

A tongue-in-cheek ode

Oh ye men who would be warriors…

Mount thy stallions   *stallions = ride-on mowers*

and do battle with the infidel green!

Bring her to heel. Remind her of her place in the mechanical conformity of things.

Teach her obedience. Leave nothing but stubble, singed roots, and elemental sorrow.

Oh ye men who would be warriors…

Unsheathe thy swords   *swords = weed whackers*

and give chase to the verdant Queen!

Behead her consorts. Castigate her for ruining the rigorous perfection of straight lines.

Scalp her silly. For land, like outspoken women, must be brought to know their place.

If you do this thing,

you will reap your reward in heaven!   *heaven = Tim Horton's drive through*

Conversely, you could take up seed and hoe and make food, not war.

---

*Thanks to Bruce Wark for the title, "Lawns and Order"

LETTER TO RACHEL ON HER BIRTHDAY
May 27, 2018

Copernicus issued a challenge.

Threatened by the Catholic Church, he didn't publish.

Carson issued a warning.

Threatened by the Capitalist Church, she published anyway.

Dear Ms. Carson,

At the risk of sounding like a gushing girl I must say your book, "Silent Spring" opened the portals of my mind to the wonders of biodiversity and the terrible price we are exacting from She who conceived, gestated and birthed us into BEING.

I'll be honest, Rachel (my apologies if it is presumptuous to call you by your first name), I often have to close these same mental portals to block out the:

> *incessant screaming of the forest as she is clear cut;*

> *holy terror in the eyes of children who know their future is foreshadowed in flood and fire;*

> *unholy howling of the last wolf in the province as he bleeds out on the barren forest floor, barren because of blatant, bilious fatuity.*

You spoke about such fatuity in your book, but I am sorry to say that despite your warnings, much of what you predicted and more has come to pass. So on behalf of the no longer wild West, and in gratitude for your brave and brilliant heart, on this, your one-hundred and twelfth birthday, I would like to dedicate this poem to you. It's called "Silent Summer".

Yours in deepest respect,

SILENT SUMMER: An Ode to the Pollinators

For three score years, as spring to summer flamed, I have *delighted*
to witness your yearly dance over fields lush with

                                        dandelion and daisy,
                                        goldenrod and milkweed,
                                        the prickly beauty of scotch thistle.

As progress lock-stepped forward, these fields slowly waned as
pesticides and suburban sprawl decimated fields once thick with

                                        cockleburs and pussy-willows,
                                        tansy and wild sage,
                                        the elegant looping of purple vetch.

Driven by dogged desperation, I conjured for you
wildish gardens, variegated mosaics of   sweet alyssum and bee balm
                                        echinacea and butterfly weed, and
                                        a talisman for your protection, wild clover.

And each summer,
to my unabridged and wholehearted delight, you came,
a fluttering, buzzing, wing-singing force, sometimes hundreds strong!

When, in these last years, your numbers dwindled,
I planted more clover!

But this year, as spring to summer flamed,
I spied with my sorrowful eye only   eight butterflies,
                                        ten honey bees,
                                        two ruby-throateds, humming,
                                        one lone bumble, aimlessly buzzing.

Without the gentle *whiiir* of your fluttering, buzzing wings,
the summer is not the same.

How long, my beloved friends until,
like the American Chestnut Moth   you are gone?

                                                        Silent summer,

                                                        SILENT—

BREAKING NEWS!
2018 HURRICANE SEASON COMMENCES EARLY

Cut to beach at Joggins.

Cue chisel-faced news anchor.

> We take you now to Joggins Fossil Cliffs where yesterday the newly installed metal staircase was torn from its moorings by hurricane force winds and a massive storm surge. Staff described the metal stairs "ripping apart like a zipper". By morning they were gone without a trace!
>
> For all you eager Superstorm-trackers, you'll be happy to know that with greenhouse gases disrupting the jet stream and warming the poles, storms that wreak havoc as did this weather event at Joggins will very soon no longer be confined to a single season!!!
>
> And now we take you to the Yucatan Peninsula for the continued coverage of Sub-tropical Storm Alberto.
>
> For the Superstorm Station, I am meat-eater-ologist, Daniel D. Niar."

And cut.

SUMMER SOLSTICE SABBAT
June 21, 2018

Morning

On this day of the longest night, my friend Elaine comes for tea.

She tells me about dragonflies, how most of their life is spent in nymph stage.

Is this long larval gestation the reason for Dragonfly's evolutionary longevity?

For like the cliffs, they claim ancestry that goes back three hundred million years.

Afternoon

I am a dragonfly nymph impatiently awaiting my metamorphosis.

Evening

I honour the thorn and the blood-coloured rose.

My heart full of visions, I chant:

> *Star light, star bright,*
> *First star I see tonight,*
> *I wish I may, I wish I might,*
> *have the wish I wish tonight.*

Raven appears to tell me my wish is granted, that I am called back to Joggins and the cliffs!

Like the God Lugh on his White Charger, I rise up,
gathering invisible weapons of heart and mind.

The clouds open their arms, revealing the constellation Ursa Major.

The bear leaves her home in the Corona Borealis.

The hunt begins.

Pattering rain made sharp by Wind stirs Fundy's waves to tiaras of foamy white.
A shiver of anticipation snakes up my spine.

I slowly make my way down to the beach and, with each step,
feel closer to a previously unknowable but yet very real *something* that is waiting to meet me.

Falcon sweeps the sky and a low hum rises up from the cliffs.
A wraith of dense fog rises around me, melts into my pores,
guides me towards the cliff face, now emanating a strange orange light.

Placing my hands on Palaeozoic rock, I feel… *What?*
Her breathing body?
Her beating heart?

Spreading wide my arms,
I release my weight to the cliff face,
feeling myself like the Medieval Abbess Heloise
as she prostrated herself on the cold marble of the chapel where she long ago served as
Mother in a Sacred Sisterhood of Christ's
now forgotten
Love.

Tears score my face. A dragonfly lands on my shoulder.
Brushing the side of my neck with lace-like wings,
She whispers,

> *Love can never be forgotten. She serenades you even now in Sacred Song.*
> *Do you not hear it? Love sung by Sea and Sky and Stone?*
> *A primordial chorus of*   *Harmony woven from*
> *Chaos then steeped in*
> *Wonder?*

Pressing myself further into ridges of limestone, shale, and slate, I open my ears.
First silence, then
multiple layers of harmonic vibration ring through the rock as the primordial chorus *huummms*.

Dragonfly regards me with her massive globular eyes.

> *I am Dragonfly, considered by some to be a symbol of transformation.*
> *Where you now stand was once the Heart of Pangea.*
> *Will you come with me? Back to the days of my ancestors to find the wisdom you seek?*
> *Quickly now, you must choose for my life span is short and I am gifting it to you.*

Wise in the ways of patience, Falcon rests on an outcrop above my head.
The Gull family hovers low, whispering their encouragement.

The hum of the primordial chorus ebbs and flows.
I utter a tentative   *yes*

The hum crescendos and with my head now spinning,
Raven jeers his impatience   *I knew you'd chicken out!*

Not one to refuse a challenge,
I shout with bravura   *Yes!*
and find I mean it.

I am Joyce's *Molly Bloom* crying to her lover
and my heart is going like mad as I say

> *Yes! Yes, I will!*
> *A thousand times, YES!!!*

No sooner are the words are out of my mouth than I find myself shrinking,
like Gulliver in the land of the giants.

As I diminish, Dragonfly grows until our relative sizes are inverted.

Raven picks me up by the scruff of my hoodie, plops me onto Dragonfly's turquoise-green back.
I nestle on her thorax between fore and hind wings.
Her wings blur as we lift off, the sound like the roar of a twin engine jet.

Rising through thick layers of violet mist, I hold on for dear life.
I am Thomas the Rhymer on the way to Elfland,
Dorothy whirling through the tornado on my way to OZ.

PART IV

INTO THE MIST
A Midsummer Night's Odyssey

"If I observe the microscopic state of things, then the difference between past and future vanishes."

Carlo Rovelli, PhD
On the Elastic Concept of Time

"From the shores through the ancient mist…I will take you home to eternal bliss."

Celtic Women
Tir Na Nog

Some say past, present and future co-exist.

This could explain why it seems as if no time at all has passed before we land.

When are we?

With the dulcet tones of a seasoned flight attendant, Dragonfly intones,

Welcome to Pangea. Geologic time: 310 million years ago.
We cannot stay here long:
atmospheric oxygen levels at 35% are too high for the human body.

I open my eyes, blink twice to adjust to the riot of colours,

inhale deeply the unfamiliar smells of vivifying green, the sulphuric tang of fertile rot.

What lies before me reminds me of the bayous of Mississippi, only the plants are supersized.

Groves of ferns with their feathery fronds create an understory above the swamp floor.

Horsetails wave in the wind on jointed stems poking sunwards.

Double-crowned palm trees with giant low-hanging cones

rise up on slender trunks adorned with geometric swirls.

Dragonfly interrupts my reverie.

The ferns are different from those in your garden — they reproduce by seeds, not spores.
What you identified as horsetail is actually an ancient relative called 'Calamites'.
The palms are not trees at all, but rather club mosses called 'Lycopsid.'
You may find it interesting to note that there are no grasses —
they will not appear for another two-hundred and fifty million years.

I scan the horizon, looking for anything else familiar. Looking up into the branches of the *Lycopsid*, I shudder as I see a spider big as a seal's head.

A Whip Spider, similar to one you would find in Papua, New Guinea.

Out of a thicket of *Calamites*, another gruesome creature — a giant millipede.

> *Correction. He is called 'Arthropleura'.*
> *An arthropod like myself, he holds the title of the world's largest living invertebrate.*

A small lizard scurries for cover inside a fire-scarred *Lycopsid*.

> *Not a lizard, but one of the earliest reptiles known as 'Hylonomous lyelli', ancestor to the*
> *dinosaurs that will be the dominant land species in one hundred million years.*
> *For scientists, Hylonomous will mark the time when life emerged from water to live on land.*

I shake my head in admiration.

> *Who knew dragonflies could be so learned?*

A flash of lightning strikes a patch of ferns.
They burst into flame which, due to the high oxygen levels, spreads like the wind.

With reflexes faster than a World War II fighter pilot fleeing attack,
Dragonfly lifts off, saving us from death by conflagration.

We land on a large patch of bare rock.
My heart is in my throat and
I am wishing I could
twinkle my nose
and go home
when
the ground beneath us begins to quake.

A sonorous voice rises up from the ground.

> *Though we of the rock world are not fixated on names or gender in the way of your kind,*
> *you may call me Stone Mother.*

My brain struggles to come to terms with a talking rock.
Dragonfly curls her tail up, taps me on the back.
I stammer a timid hello.

> *I have been with you in the days of future passed,*
> *will be with you in the future that has yet to come.*
> *I understand you have come seeking wisdom.*
> *As an offering of gratitude, I will accept the white feathers from your headdress.*

With shaking hands, I pull them from my hair,
loose them gently onto the Stone Mother's back.

> *Ah, how beautiful. Now…listen carefully.*
> *You are relative newcomers to Earth.*
> *Your first 198,000 years showed promise.*
> *You walked on my back honouring the Divine Energies of the Four Elements.*
> *As your collective strength grew, you flourished: quite the accomplishment*
> *for creatures with no fur for warmth, no fangs or claws for protection,*
> *not to mention that you weren't particularly fleet of foot.*
> *We of the rock world were eager to see where your big brains would take you.*
> *Alas, almost to the edge of doom, it seems.*
> *You are called Homo Sapiens: Sapien being Latin for "Wise."*
> *But those dominant among you used your adaptive abilities to your disadvantage,*
> *and thus you buried your wisdom in the quest for Empire.*
> *Allow me to elaborate.*

EMPIRE

Eden
Maliciously manipulated,
Pagan practices purposefully
Incinerated to be replaced by deadening ideologies
Replete with righteous assertions of egregious
Entitlement. You have perfected the philosophy of

Existential idiocy,
Making death from the numinous as you chant, "I want…I need…I have the right to
Play God Almighty!" You congeal Creation! Rape and revile! Irradiate
Innocence! What is required here? A revolution waged not with guns but
Rooted in your forgotten relationship with all Life! Do this and you can
Expect our unqualified support. Choose to ignore this by staying in your collective

Eggshells, infatuated with the trancelike spell your puppet masters have induced and the
Mass putrefaction of the great vision of your kind will continue as you knowingly
Poison that which sustains you! What makes you think that
I the Rock, I the Air, I the Water, and I the Fire that burns
Radiant at the planet's core will not allow your
Extinction?

E for EXTINCT   or
E for ETERNAL   YOUR CHOICE!

I feel queasy.

I don't like being so small.

Dragonfly bows, and in silence we fly away.

It appears the audience with Stone Mother is over.

The light is fading as we fly over a canopy of *Lycopsid* before landing again.

As I release my grip on Dragonfly's back, she begins to flit:

up and down, down and up, and as I am unused to bronco riding, I soon find myself airborne.

A high whining sound fills my ears as I land

flat on my back in a pile of dirt which, like Zarathustra, speaks:

> *I am Dirt!*
>
> *You use my name as a put-down, but hey man, wise up!*
>
> *In my atmosphere lives a riot of riches beyond compare:*
>
> *fungi and mites, pollen and bacteria, and other cool beings without which*
>
> > *Life as you know it,*
> >
> > *Life as we grow it will perish!*
> >
> > *Can you dig it?*
>
> *Hmmm…that was a joke.*
>
> *Y'all need to lighten up.*
>
> *I'll get straight to the point.*
>
> *Go back to your time and repair me!*
>
> *Go back to your time and declare me   King! Or Queen! or*
>
> > *His Royal Blackesty!*
>
> *Hell, the title doesn't matter, only the esteem.*
>
> *Remember, what you've destroyed, you can heal.*
>
> *Honouring Dirt — a simple shortcut from stupidity to sanity!*

I pull Falcon's feathers from my hair, lay them in Dirt's mound-like hand.

Hey…if you don't mind, I want the black feather.
It blends better with my ensemble, if you catch my particle drift!

I am pondering the question of how to get back up onto Dragonfly's back when
Arthropleura slithers out of a thicket of *Calamites*   on his hundreds of legs
                                                                                   as big as a crocodile,
                                                                                   and I the size of a pygmy mouse.
Powered by a mainline hit of adrenaline,
in the style of Olympic gymnast, Mary Lou Retton, I do a run-skip-JUMP!
that lands me squarely between Dragonfly's wings.

    I'm impressed! I'd suggest we hang around so you can dazzle me with other feats of
    human strength, but time is running out and I have one more introduction to make that
    requires us to return to the future. Plus you are looking a bit twitchy. Probably too much oxygen.

We lift off.
Unlike the journey here which was painless, the journey back is agony.
Knife-sharp pains cascade through my body and I am praying for a speedy death when
finally, mercifully, I black out.

I come to consciousness to find myself falling,
       free falling and picking up speed, going faster and faster through white space,
              like a recurring nightmare I've had since childhood, except I know this is real,
                     as real as a journey through time on the back of a Dragonfly can be.

I land with a thud on something hard and flat.

Opening my eyes, vertigo hits.

I am some six hundred feet atop the tallest of three red stones high over Chignecto Bay.

> Looking down, I see a wall of water rising, then crashing up against the rocks far below.
> Dragonfly, now no longer a giant, comes to rest on my shoulder.

> *The Red Rhyolite rock on which you sit on is four hundred million years old.*
> *It embodies the spirit beings known to the Mi'kmaq as "Siknikt"*
> *also known as "The Three Sisters."*
> *Listen well and learn.*

> *The time has come for me to bid you good-bye.*
> *You must make this last leg of the journey on your own.*

And then she is gone.

A chorus of voices speaking as one envelopes me.

> *We are the Three Sisters of the Wabanaki Nation.*
> *In the time of Legendary Kluscap, we were Puowi-ni'skw — shapeshifters.*
> *But when we began to abuse our power, Kluscap, being wise,*
> *put a stop to our mischief by turning us into stone.*

> *Your kind has abused its power.*
> *You are lucky Kluscap still sleeps.*

A jet flies overhead, the noise painful after the Carboniferous quiet.

The Three Sisters continue…

All life is related, and rock is not a dead thing.

    We are close cousins to the   *Three Sisters Rocks in the Land of the Navajo*
                                          Three Sisters Rocks of the Gundungura People
                                            Three Sisters of Corn, Beans and Squash
                                            that are sacred to my people.

    We are also related to the   *Three Sisters of Past, Present, and Future*
                                            Three Domains of Life — Bacteria, Archaea, and Eurcarya
                                            Sacred Trinity of Maiden, Mother, and Crone that comes
                                            from your ancestral lore.

    As you can see, we like patterns of three. Do you know any more?

Childhood memories snap into frame. Storytime in Grandma's arms listening to
                              The Three Little Pigs
                              The Three Bears
                              The Woodsman's Three Wishes

And later, ensconced in the library, reading everything I can find on
                              The Three Brontë Sisters — Emily, Charlotte and Anne
                              The Three Warrior Women — Tomoe Gozen, Joan of Arc,
                                      and Boudicca of the Iceni
                              Chekhov's three Prozorov sisters — Olga, Masha and Irina

    Masha: *We must live!*

    Irina: *A time will come when everyone will know…why there is all this suffering…*

    Olga: *Oh my dear sisters…it seems as if just a little more, and we shall know why we live, why we suffer. If only we knew. If only we knew.*

Sun begins to set over blue-green water.
The Three Sisters Rocks sigh... *If only you knew...*

In the changing light, over red rhyolite
now a majestic magenta, Falcon sails in... *If only you knew...*

Raven rockets up from a crag of rock below, and
Laughing Gulls seemingly fly out of nowhere... *If only you knew...*

Quickly removing the two golden feathers from my former crown,
I tuck them into a crevice of the tallest of the Sisters.

They are at once alight their voices ringing out a pure flowering green!

This from the People of the Dawn...

Offer gifts
Humble yourselves
Listen more than talk
Don't take yourselves so seriously
Take very seriously your commitment to She who is our Mother
Make amends to those you have injured
Find your place in the Circle of Living Things
Practice two-eyed seeing*

Do these things, and your kind will find their way.
This is the promise of the Three Sisters.

Now...trust that your Life will not fail you, and leap!

I leap!

    Only to find I am not flying, but falling,

        tumbling through the air helter-skelter,

            down, down, down towards the shimmering waters.

                    …trust that your Life will not fail you…

I am falling, crying, trusting I am dying when around me, wildly winging

    Falcon, Raven and my trio of Laughing Gulls!

    Then, within me, joyously singing, the Three Sisters,

        Stone Mother, and laying on a kickin' harmony, His Royal Blackesty!

                    …trust that your Life will not fail you…

I am trusting,

    trusting and falling,

        falling then…

            flying, lifted on the wings of pure ecstasy!

                    …trust that your Life will not fail you…

I am Sophia carrying the Soul of the World!

    I am Jesus' little sister walking on turbulent waters!

        I am the Light that burns at the end of the Tunnel!

                    …trust that your Life will not fail you…

and now I *am* the Tunnel…no
    am *in* the tunnel, and *oh*
    it is *squeeeeezing* me, *oh*
    the pain…I wish I…*OH*
    there is no "I", only pulsing,
    squeezing, *seeaaaring*, supernova pain, *ooh* and now
    there are sure hands guiding me, *ooh* and now
    a reassuring voice calming me, *ooooh* and now
    in a *whoosh* of salty fluid,
    I slide out
        head first,
            slick and sticky,
                landing face down on the ground
                    on morning warmed sand
                        safe by the cliffs at Joggins.

---

* Two-eyed seeing: A concept developed by Mi'kmaq Elder, Albert Marshall as part of an integrative approach to science. One eye sees using the strength of Indigenous ways of knowing, while the other eye sees through the strengths of Western ways of knowing. Eventually both eyes are used together for the benefit of all Creation.

PART V

A REBIRTH OF WONDER

"We are a vast web of interconnected relationships, where every single thought and action is felt by all of the other pieces of the web. Each of us is part of the whole where no act is insignificant. We have a responsibility to the whole. Not only are we in relationship to all life, we are actually a relative to all life."

Pam Montgomery
Partner Earth

"…even the tiniest bacteria has zero respect for impossibility."

Dr. Stephen Harding
Deep Time Walk

"…and I am perpetually awaiting a rebirth of wonder."

Lawrence Ferlinghetti
A Coney Island of the Mind

HARVEST FESTIVAL OF LAMMAS
August 1, 2018
Celebrating the Goddess and the Green Man

On this day, as my ancestors harvested
wheat and barley, oats, and rye,
meadowsweet, mint, and calendula
they gave thanks for their daily bread
(something I often take for granted).

A spirit wind blows,
and for an eternal moment,
I am once again riding on the back of Dragonfly in a long ago time.

With a heart overflowing I throw sprigs of
peppermint, summer sage, and purple crowned yarrow
into the wind
into the water
into the fecund mud.

Bowing, I offer tears of thanks
to the trickster wisdom of the blue-black Raven
the unfettered joy of the family of Gulls
the serene majesty of Falcon.

I follow the tide out until I can no longer move, my feet sunk calf-high in mud.

Turning to hail the cliffs one last time, I fall ass-over-tea-kettle into the rubbery clay.

Raven sniggers, then chortles.

Falcon guffaws, and the Gulls join in, and before long, I too am howling in unfettered glee.

Later, as I pull my mud-encrusted body up the newly installed stairs

I spy a world-weary woman leading a gaggle of preschoolers down the hill.

As I watch the little flock of human ducklings waddle and *quack* towards me,

my face splits from ear to ear and I call out a greeting.

Seeing me covered in muck with my hair sticking out at all angles, they stop.

Mother Duck shoots me a killing glare as she corrals her brood to scurry past me.

With a start, I realize I know her and *quack* her name.

Hesitantly, she turns. Her eyes flash recognition.

Her pink-stained lips open into a smile,

I invite her and the baby ducks to join me in song.

> *The happy Mother Duck goes*   quack, quack, quack
>   quack, quack, quack
>   quack, quack, quack…

As she sings, the mask of long suffering drops from her face.

> *The happy Mother Duck goes*   quack, quack, quack…

Gone are years of strain and worry as she and her brood lift their voices.

A Mallard family flying overhead join in, and around the cliffs our voices ring…

> *all around the town!*

> Humans and ducks singing together!
> *A first step towards world peace?*

THE MABON
September 21, 2018

Honour the changing seasons
Reap what you have sown

Sunset on the beach at Joggins.

Sky is a canvas of scarlet and persimmon shot through with brushstrokes of amber and grey.

The tide is tumbling inland with upstart waves the colour of slate careening to shore.

The gusting wind is both a sob and an exultation.

carrying the bitterness of healing medicine forged in a crucible of loss.

The cliffs, cloaked in amber mist, whisper,

Remember,

every day you must give your love to the world,

for she needs you to see her beauty,

cry her tears of sorrow for all that is lost that can never again be found.

You are her heart.

You are her hands.

You are her voice.

And don't forget, if it ever feels too much, come back to us.

We of the rock world have a few tricks hidden up our sedimentary sleeves

and the ending to your story is not yet written.

Dare to hope.

Three hundred million years ago on the supercontinent of Pangea,
Life conspired with Rock, Sea, and Sky to dream a grand experiment.
And so it follows that
like the flow of Fundy's tidal bore,
the Green Language of our young Ivan,
and the sweet whisperings of my beloved Weeping Willow,
I, too, am Pangea's Dream.

Yes, I, the patience of the seed who trusts the Dreamer's growing need
to gestate in her womb of dark and thus distil a silent spark of
Wonder,
rend asunder
this empirical nightmare scheme!

Yes, I, the thousand winds that blow,
I, the silent evening glow,
I, the pebble in the stream,
I, the sunlight's constant beam,
I, the rainbow in the sky,
I, the tears of those who cry,
I, the bursting leaves of spring,
I, the song the green woods sing!

Yes, I am Pangaea's dream.
Whose dream are you?

EPILOGUE

O Great Dreamer

Who art our Eternal Mother,

Hallowed by thy Flame.

Thy Rapture come,

Thy Songs be sung

In Joy at thy Simple Wonder.

Give us this day our daily Breath

And forgive us our Hubris

As we forgive that which makes us Complicit.

And leave us not lost in Benumbment,

But deliver us from Extinction.

For Thine is the History, the Mystery and the Morrow

Forever and ever.

And so it is.

AFTERWORD

RAPALLO, ITALY
November 2018

Nestled on the edge of the Ligurian Sea, the medieval Commune of Rapallo.

Here, Hannibal prepared to do battle with the Romans after crossing the Alps.

Here, the Pagan Goddess Diana was recast as the Archangel Michael.

Here, Nietzsche, Yeats and Pound walked the waterfront and mused their masterpieces,

and though I came to follow in their august footsteps,

I instead arrived to witness a scene of Anthropocene carnage.

Strewn at the edge of the piazza, a mishmash of refuse and ruin.

Gale force winds and ten meter high waves had battered the coast for days,

breaking down the reinforced concrete seawall and sinking two hundred sailing vessels.

Out in the harbour, thirty-foot catamarans, half-submerged, were slowly sinking.

At the harbour's edge, five hundred foot yachts lay shipwrecked,

as if Poseidon himself had risen in giant form to effortlessly hurl them landward.

Further down the bay, the lifeless bodies of porpoises littered the shore;

their frolicking songs forever stilled.

The Castle by the Sea, built in 1551 to warn of frequent pirate attacks was still standing,

and the medieval stone walkways had suffered little damage—

a compelling illustration of the value of workmanship over speed of completion.

Rapallo is five thousand, five hundred and seventy-four kilometres from the cliffs at Joggins.

In Pangea, it would have been just a jaunt down the road, a close second cousin as rock relations go—

a compelling illustration of how Carbon Age rock continues to bear witness.

LAMENTATION FOR WATER

The Grandmother of all sentient life is the Ocean.
Plundered and poisoned, she is renitent now—
Salacia's last stand.

Along her once-lush, now-barren shores   the sons stand stoic while
                                          the daughters heap their heads with dust while
                                          the elders keep the silence.

A watery sun rises in the blood-dimmed sky
as from parched throats we cry as one...

> *O Beloved, who art the Ocean*
> *Forgive us.*

The grandmother of all life on Earth is the Ocean.
Once home of Hina Moa, Neptune and the Goddess Yemaya—
She is dying now.
Within her once-fecund, now beggared realm   the green cells atrophy while
                                              the whale keens her last while
                                              a one hundred and twenty-year-old turtle
                                              sinks like stone, his guts splintered with plastic.

A pale moon canters in a green-grey sky
as the shifting tides glow with uranium.

> *O Beloved, who art the Ocean*
> *Forgive us.*

KLUSCAP'S SORROW

Dedicated to my daughter, who knows.

The learned speaker takes the stage, clears his throat,

"We stand on unceded Mi'kmaq land and we *honour* your culture and traditions."

> The speaker has forgotten.
> *Honour* is a verb.

The right honourable Prime Minister calls a press conference, adjusts his tie,

"We honour our First Peoples and we *apologize* for centuries of colonial violence."

> The Prime Minister has forgotten.
> *Apologize* is a verb.

Say one thing, then do another.   Like my father, tipped the bottle, said
"I love you," before he raised his hand.

(Translation: "I hurt you, I'll do it again, but sorry...")

Say one thing, then do another.   The Lords of Conquest soon discovered,
promise *honour* before you rape the land.

(Translation: "We took your land, we're not giving it back, but hey...sorry for that thing with the smallpox blankets.")

> Kluscap's Sorrow

SEVEN GENERATION THINKING

We overcome the eddies of gloom that snag our thoughts in a downward spiral

by radiating possibility.

We treat the poison of prevailing apathy

by taking measured, wholehearted action towards accessing our collective birthright.

In its death throes, the patriarchy

is exercising its only remaining power: the power to destroy.

But given time and our willing help,

Nature can reclaim her dead places and the soil will once again

hum with the community of living organisms.

The remaining ancient forests will stand with us in solidarity.

> To hell with the hero's journey!
> No one person can save us now.

Published in the online journal "What Rough Beast" / Indolent Books, April 2018

WIND IN THE SKY

Dedicated to my Grandmother, Christine Haines Paddon, my mentor, Marie-Louise Simich and all the Wyse Wymen who have gone before who honoured the ways of listening

In the chill of November, the beauty of May,
be it city or forest, she finds her way.
Hear the dawn's hush in winter,
see the moon in her eyes,
her map, the aurora,
or as the crow flies.
The cold wind blows gentle as she brushes the lie
from a wilderness crying, it's wisdom denied.
The great Oak remembers the strength of her kind.
She listens and follows the wind in the sky.

Her hair streaked with silver flows thick down her back
each strand tells a story of glory and lack,
of laughter and sorrow,
of love, here then gone,
a life richly woven,
a full-throated song.
She sings of the babies she's caught that survived,
She keens with the night wind for those that have died.
And she prays as she runs as the moon rises high,
She listens and follows the wind in the sky.

The shadows they fall away,

fall away dancing,

Her heartbeat says

fly away…fly on the owl's wing!

Be one with the pulse of the wandering deer!

The Birch tree births memory, her vision comes clear.

I carry the blood of the Old Ones, says she

to the towering forest, the depths of the sea,

and the night bird wings homeward

as the whippoorwill cries,

I listen and follow the wind in the sky.

Today you may see her in the rise of the sun,

the halls of the city,

a life's work well done.

Let the dark night embrace you and you will see her face

in all creatures, all families,

the whole human race.

Rejoice sons and daughters like a child in the spring!

As the Mystery deepens, the Universe sings.

I am here now within you,

and as night draws nigh,

just listen and follow the wind in the sky,

just listen and follow the wind in the sky,

just listen and follow,

follow,

follow the wind…

First published in the journal "The Lorelei Signal" / WolfSinger Press, San Diego, 2009

GUEST POETS OF
THE JOGGINS PROJECT

UNDERCURRENTS
Heather Payne

Be not afraid of the undercurrents

Stirring, brewing beneath the

Surface: swirling waves

Pushing

Pulling

Grains of sand

Wood that drifts

Bottle glass with abrasive edges yet to be eroded.

Be not afraid of the undercurrents

Step out in confidence

As roaring whitecaps

Beat against

Thrash against

Life's shores!

Through the misty haze

Wounds heal, and though scars remain,

Grace emerges.

Expect the unexpected

Fulfillment

Be not afraid of the undercurrents.

Heather Payne is a retired resident of Wood Point, New Brunswick who enjoys volunteer work, reading, writing, gardening and painting. Married to Michael, with two daughters Jessica and Melissa, she has always enjoyed writing.

AT THE TORN EDGE
Cynthia McCarthy

At the torn edge of time
Sky and earth and tide spin a dance

    Mesmeric—through pearly mist, the distant cape steps forth

    throws off the veils and casts,

    from far beyond her hills, the boreas -

    upswept when soon it meets these ancient cliffs.

    The solemn turf now wakes to join!

    Spring's pliant grasses held secure,

    yet bow their heads and reach in backward allemande

    accordant with the squall;

    Now all the moon-struck basin

    whips and whirls;

    Now heady wavelets, flush of muddied roses,

    thrash exultant!

Meanwhile

These ribbons of melting stone

Abide

In rapt observance.

Now living in Fort Lawrence, with deep roots on the South Shore of Nova Scotia, Cynthia McCarthy enjoyed a long career in Visual Arts education. Most recently her interests are painting, printmaking and photographing the little moments.

JOGGINS, THIRTY-ONE YEARS ON
Carolynn Lunn

Water
    Cascades over
    Carboniferous cliffs, a
Clattering
    Cacophony on
    Crumbled remnants of a long ago age.
Liquid ribbons
    Lash sideways in the
    Ever-present wind as
Braided channels
    rush to embrace the waves.

Grappling with the gale
Grounded   in this moment,
        in this place,
I journey to another time, when
        fresh from tearful torrents,
I sought solace on this strand, and felt the healing
    Balm of
        Wind
            and
                Waves
                    and
                        Stone

Originally from Mahone Bay, Nova Scotia, Carolyn Lunn is a retired speech-language pathologist currently living in Smiths Falls, Ontario. Despite moving away in 1979, she continues to consider Nova Scotia home, returning yearly to visit family and relax by the sea.

ACKNOWLEDGEMENTS

Many thanks to everyone at the Joggins Fossil Institute: especially Education and Outreach Manager, Laurie Glenn Norris; Curator of Paleontology, Dr. Melissa Grey; and Director of Administration, Lorna Terrio; as well as *Artscape* and the Municipality of the County of Cumberland (Nova Scotia) for funding support.

Working with Keith, Ellen, and Brendan Helmuth at Chapel Street Editions has been an important part of this project. Keith is a lifelong warrior for truth and justice and it has meant the world to collaborate on *Daring to Hope at the Cliff's Edge* with a man who lives and breathes his politics. Thanks also to Ellen for bringing a keen eye for proofing to the mix, and Brendan for such a superb job on laying out this work with attention to the narrative—I know it was not easy.

I am grateful to Cree/Metis scholar Dr. Paulette Steeves and Mi'kmaq Elders Louise Goodwin and Emile Gautreau for offering feedback on my use of Indigenous references. *Miigwetch.* Any errors are my own.

I will be forever indebted to Dr. Robert Lapp who offered the kind of invaluable insights that can only come from a scholar who lives and breathes poetry.

Some of the poems in this work had their genesis in the 2017 spoken-word play, "Bearing Witness," and here I acknowledge the support of Mount Allison University as well as Canadian Playwright, Sharon Pollock who encouraged me to trust my voice as a writer no matter what the genre.

I need solitude to write so big thanks to the following Scotians who opened their homes for free: the late Su Morin and the dynamic duo of musicians Colleen Collins and Dave Trenaman from Port Greville; Courtney Trowse and family from Shad Bay; Lee Ann McKoy from River Hebert; Dr. Helen Douglas and Tedward the horse from Baie Verte, New Brunswick.

As part of my residency, I facilitated a poetry writing workshop from which came three excellent poems. Many thanks to Heather Payne, Carolyn Lunn, and Cynthia McCarthy for agreeing to allow their inclusion in this book.

A shout out to friends who saw me through countless iterations of this narrative poem, including but not limited to: Sackville's former Poet Laureate, Marilyn Lerch, Janet Thom Hammock, Judith Weiss, Michael Fox, Margaret Tusz-King, Janice and Ron Melanson, Heather Payne, Laura Penney, Colleen Collins, Rachael Numidia and Leah Alexandra Huff. A big *Eeechup!* to author Deborah Carr for sharing her knowledge of bird lore at the exact time I needed it.

Where would I be without family and close friends? To my Aunt Kat, thanks for providing me with the critical information I needed about Grandpa Balfour; the poem 'Remembrance Day' is richer as a result. To my best friends for life, Marion Law and Shelley Hamilton—your love and encouragement have grounded me through this past difficult but inspiring year. To my sister, Mary Armellini—your integrity and fierce loyalty have been a blessed constant in a turbulent life. To my daughter, Faith Chaput—simply put, you lift me in love.

None of this would be possible without my husband, Beverly Glenn-Copeland. Honey, I could not have seen this process through without your support, not to mention your willingness to be banned from the house when I was writing!

In closing...

An abundance of gratitude for the wisdom teachings of the Fossil Cliffs, the mighty Bay of Fundy, and the winged creatures who became my particular friends over the course of this project.

To all my relations, be you rooted or winged, two, four or multi-legged, I see you.

To the Great Dreamer who dreamed us to life, I offer my heart.

And I am listening.

ABOUT THE AUTHOR

Elizabeth Glenn-Copeland is an award-winning author, theatre artist, storyteller and arts educator. In her younger days, she performed on stages throughout North America. Her hands down favourite role was the *Witch* in *Hansel and Gretel* with the Honolulu Symphony. Her literary work has been published in *The Furious Gazelle, Circa — A Journal of Historical Fiction,* and *Forge Journal*, among others. Elizabeth won the 2014 Writers Federation of New Brunswick Young Adult Fiction Award for an excerpt from *Traeh Gnul — Miranda's Journey from the Great Forest. JAZZ — Nature's Improvisation* won 2014 Ken Klonsky Novella Prize and was shortlisted for the 2015 ReLit Award. With her composer husband, Beverly Glenn-Copeland, she has co-written, directed and produced a number of musical plays including *The Raven of Eirean Mohr*.

Over the past two decades, Elizabeth has rooted her artistic practice in a commitment to environmental and social justice. With support from Mount Allison University, she wrote and performed the spoken-word eco-play, *Bearing Witness,* and launched the first phase of the Earth Warriors Theatre Project. In recognition of these community-based works she was given the local 2018 *Environmental Leadership Award*. Elizabeth currently lives in the town of Sackville, N.B. with her husband and two cats. *Daring to Hope at the Cliff's Edge* is her debut book of poetry.

SELECTED REFERENCES

Abram, David. *The Spell of the Sensuous: Perception and Language in a More-than-Human World*. Vintage Books / Random House, Inc., 2017.

"A Story with Heart and Soil." *Dirt The Movie The Filmmakers Comments*, www.dirtthemovie.org/.

Biello, David. *The Unnatural World: the Race to Remake Civilization in Earths Newest Age*. Scribner, 2017.

Burzynski, Michael, and Anne Marceau. *Fundy, Bay of the Giant Tides*. Fundy Guild, 2011.

Calder, John. *The Joggins Fossil Cliffs: Coal Age Galápagos*. Formac, 2017.

Castello, Molly S. "Coming to Terms With Eco-anxiety." *Psychology Today*, Sussex Publishers, http://www.psychologytoday.com/us/blog/the-me-in-we/201801/coming-terms-ecoanxiety.

Estés, Clarissa Pinkola. *Women Who Run with the Wolves: Contacting the Power of the Wild Woman*. Rider, 1996.

Eisler, Riane. *Real Wealth of Nations*. Berrett-Koehler Publishers, 2008.

Falcon-Lang, Howard J., et al. "Joggins, Nova Scotia." *Geology Today*, vol. 26, no. 3, 2010, 114., doi:10.1111/j.1365-2451.2010.00755.x.

Federici, Silvia. *Caliban and the Witch*. Autonomedia, 2014.

Gilding, Paul. *Great Disruption: Why the Climate Crisis Will Bring on the End of Shopping and the Birth of a New World*. Bloomsbury, 2012.

Higgins, Charlotte. "'There Is No Such Thing as Past or Future:' Physicist Carlo Rovelli on Changing How We Think about Time." *The Guardian*, Guardian News and Media, 14 Apr. 2018, www.theguardian.com/books/2018/apr/14/carlo-rovelli-exploding-commonsense-notions-order-of-time-interview.

Loye, David. *Darwin's Lost Theory: Who We Really Are and Where Were Going*. Benjamin Franklin Press, 2007.

Macy, Joanna, and Chris Johnstone. *Active Hope: How to Face the Mess Were in without Going Crazy*. New World Library, 2012.

Mi'kmawey Debert Cultural Centre. www.mikaweydebert.ca/home/

Montgomery, Pam. *Partner Earth: a Spiritual Ecology*. Destiny Books, 1997.

Norris, Laurie Glenn. *Cumberland County: Facts and Folklore*. Nimbus, 2012.

Parrish, Judith Totman. "Climate of the Supercontinent Pangea." *The Journal of Geology*, vol. 101, no. 2, 1993, pp. 215–233., doi:10.1086/648217.

Pennick, Nigel. *The Pagan Book of Days: a Guide to the Festivals, Traditions, and Sacred Days of the Year*. Destiny Books, 2001.

Raffi, and Sharna Olfman. *Child Honoring: How to Turn This World Around*. Homeland Press, 2010.

Starhawk. *Dreaming the Dark: Magic, Sex, and Politics*. Beacon Press, 1997.

"Two-Eyed Seeing." *Guiding Principles (Two Eyed Seeing) | Integrative Science*, www.integrativescience.ca/Principles/TwoEyedSeeing/.

Thurston, Harry. *Tidal Life: a Natural History of the Bay of Fundy*. Nimbus, 1998.

Van Gelder, Sonya. "Ancient Wisdom". *Ancient Wisdom*, 2019, https://www.ancientwisdomoftheancestors.com/language-of-the-birds.

Ywahoo, Dhyani, and Barbara Du Bois. *Voices of Our Ancestors: Cherokee Teachings from the Wisdom Fire*. Shambhala,1987.

www.ingramcontent.com/pod-product-compliance
Lightning Source LLC
Chambersburg PA
CBHW081403070526
44583CB00020B/2661